Beautifully Convoluted

An honest look at the daily hurdles
we face as women and confronting them
with the word of God.

Chris Forkuo

ISBN 978-1-0980-0416-3 (paperback)
ISBN 978-1-0980-0457-6 (digital)

Christian Faith Publishing, Inc.
832 Park Avenue
Meadville, PA 16335
www.christianfaithpublishing.com

Printed in the United States of America

Contents

The technical definition of convoluted is, "intricately folded, twisted, or coiled." I can't think of a better definition to define us as women. We are so beautifully convoluted! We are intricately folded in our thinking, with our emotions and with our feelings. It's important to recognize this in our journey and not look at it as a bad thing, but rather a beautiful thing that we can embrace and almost confront confidently to ourselves. Every day we have the choice to allow God to lead. But how do we do that? Throughout this journal, I will walk through *every day hurdles* that we face as women and note answers in scripture that take authority over those hurdles.

I will tell you about my personal hurdles and the scriptures that I have leaned on for clarity and direction.

Every single day, *things* will try to cloud what should be clear. There is a calling for your life and also personal desires that you have. If we allow "who we were" to define who we ARE, then we get distracted. The key to not allowing a past or present struggle to reign over your life is by knowing that God is the only one that matters, period, and by putting Him at the forefront of your mind. Additionally, especially as women, we need to be raw. Be completely and utterly honest with where you are in life and where you want to be. Do not pretend you have it all together, rather speak, "this is who I was, this is who I am and this is where I want to be," is a great starting point.

Leviticus 26:3–4 says, "If you follow my decrees and are careful to obey my commands, I will send you rain in its season, and the ground will yield its crops and the trees of the field their fruit."

What in your life do you desire? What will be "your crops yielding fruit"? For me it is financial freedom. Another desire I have is for this book to come to fruition. I woke up one year ago at 2:00 a.m.

with all of this on my heart. I wrote it all out for a few hours until I was done. I continued to work on it here and there for a year then prayed. God spoke to my heart that I needed to obey him first. What does that look like exactly? Take some time to write down some tangible goals, small or big.

About me

Astory you've heard many times. Born-again Christian at the ripe age of six. I invited Christ into my heart while my mom kneeled over my bedside and prayed the prayer of salvation with me. By the time I hit the preteen years, I was throwing away all of my secular mix music tapes after attending Christian youth conventions. I remember my older brother, who had the best collection of music, had copied his tapes for me. Anyone who is over the age of thirty knows the labor that goes into copying tapes. He spent hours recording all of his tapes onto new tapes. He bought me a new case to put them all in (there must have been thirty) and gave it to me on my birthday. I was so excited to have my own set of tapes. Then a few months later, I went to a youth convention where they taught us to abandon all things that wouldn't lead us close to God, so I threw away ALL the tapes he worked so hard to make for me. He saw them in the trash and was hurt and asked my mom why I did that. My mom tried to explain it the best she could. He must have felt very hurt when I did that. Looking back now I wish someone had explained to me that taking that action was not completely necessary. I wish I had kept those tapes.

I must laugh at my twelve-year-old self now. I was and am a very literal person. That action is a prime example of me taking instructions too literally. I was on fire and abandoning all worldly things for the Lord.

Then I went to high school. Dun-dun-duuun. We all know where this is going.

All of the sudden I was quickly swept off track and away from the Lord. He was always there, but I left. Temptation and curiosity got the best of me. I put Jesus in the closet, shut the door and walked away from about the age of sixteen to twenty-five. I chose worldly things that at the time felt good but, in the end, left me feeling empty. Shopping, drinking, going out for nice meals were all fun and are not necessarily a bad thing, but if you're finding *your whole entire identity in those things*, then you will be left feeling lost and empty. I went through high school and college this way. The fun girl. The girl that everyone wanted at every party. Cheerleader, cheer captain, college dance team, and sorority sister became my identity. It didn't take much for a guy to tell me all the right things only to leave me feeling abandoned and part of my soul chipped away at (which I didn't discover was actually happening until years later). My college friends and I would binge drink. Some of us keep in touch, and I have recently talked to one of them about it, and we are in agreement that we feel disgusted at how far we took it when we went out drinking and how that was our "normal." I was known by everyone as fun, energetic and a good friend. However, I knew me as hurt and empty. By the end of college, I felt pretty lost.

Then I was thrown a lifeline when I was twenty-five. My best friend from my elementary and youth-group days came into the picture again right when I needed her. We bumped into each other at a mutual friend's college graduation party, and she stuck to my side that summer, encouraging me as she could tell I was completely floundering and had no clue who I was. I was not the confident friend she once knew when we were young. After that summer was over, she invited me to a church service that changed my life. The pastor had a prop on the stage, a fishing rod. My best friend leaned over and whispered to me, "Oh this is going to be good, he never uses props." So I reluctantly put my listening ears on.

He told a story about how he went fishing with a friend. He tried to pull up a catch that just would not budge. With a lot of muscle power, he pulled up what he thought was going to be a monster fish on the other end of his fishing line. To his surprise he was pulling up *another* fishing rod. An old, disgusting, rusted, decrepit fishing rod that, a long time ago, someone had decided was broke and unfixable, so they tossed it into the water. It had been at the bottom of that lake for many years. He decided to take that old rod home and restore it and bring it back to new condition. His friend thought he was crazy to invest in that piece of junk.

It took him a year, but he did it. He worked on it a little bit every day and restored it to new. The shiny silver new parts and the smooth and soft sounds of a turning reel replaced the old rusted fishing rod. His friend that he had been fishing with that day, a year back, came over and said to him, "Oh you got a new fishing rod, nice!" He responded, "No, this is that old one that you told me to toss back in the water and wasn't worth bringing home." In that moment I felt like the pastor spoke directly to me and God spoke directly to my heart. I was that old rod that had been left to rust and someone decided to pick up and restore to new. They closed that service with the song "Amazing Grace" and while I sang that song, I could not hold back the tears (or the mascara). I was a beautiful mess, and it was good. From that moment on, I said to the Lord, I was ready to live for Him, no matter how many mistakes I had made or *would continue to make*, I wanted to be new again. I wanted to live for Him.

Here I am fifteen years later. Married to the man of my dreams and have two beautiful girls. I could not have imagined it then. I had never even dated a Christian guy. After I rededicated my life to the Lord and truly put Him first, there he was, my man that I had always prayed for but didn't think I deserved.

I write this book knowing that the devil would love more than anything right now for my gritty past to completely debilitate and cripple me.

I battle thoughts of feeling unworthy to even write this. I battle thoughts that people from my past probably gossip about me and probably talk about how they *know* the "real me." But let me say this, the real me is not perfect. The real me faces battles still every day, screws up often, and faces temptation. However, the difference now is I have chosen to let that go as I am reminded that God is the only one to seek approval from.

When we verbally say to the Lord, "I give this to you," we allow Him to have the control. Then by taking the next step of truly believing it in our heart and fully releasing it to him, with no timeline attached, we see freedom. I have heard people say that women think in webs, constantly take one string to another string, to another string, slowly stringing invalid thoughts together. Often, we get so caught up in this web that we do not realize we are *stuck* right in the middle, unable to find a release. That is the design of the enemy. To trap us in our thought life.

When a negative thought happens, you need to cast it down. "I do not accept that, in Jesus's name," or "God, you are in control of my life and the only one I seek approval from."

Having a conversation with your Father in Heaven is the only way to fully feel released from worry, anxiety, frustration, anger, insecurity, and the list goes on.

Now, let's get into the actual hurdles that may come your way. Step one, you will only leverage the height of a hurdle with an honest relationship with God.

There are many verses in the Bible that will help you overcome hurdles if you believe in your heart and confess with your mouth that Jesus is your Savior. Better yet you will flat out knock the hurdle over!

Romans 10:9–10 says, "That if you confess with your mouth, 'Jesus is Lord,' and believe in your heart that God raised him from the dead, you will be saved. For it is with your heart that you

believe and are justified, and it is with your mouth that you con-
fess and are saved."

What is the hurdle you are dealing with? I challenge you to search for a Bible verse to help you with that hurdle. Write your hurdle and Bible verse down in the lines provided. Take time to journal and pray.

Anger

I am trying really hard not to, but I lose my temper with my four- and six-year-old girls. I love them hard. I hug, kiss, cuddle and encourage. But I also lose my temper too often. I yell, sometimes scream, and then I break down. It happens, and it just sucks. I am blessed to have girls that love me and when I ask for forgiveness, they are always willing to and we move forward. I'm working on this, but it's a hard truth that is part of my life right now. I am choosing to seek the Lord on this and have friends pray for me because I cannot master this *mother thing* on my own.

Scripture tells us: "In your anger do not sin. Do not let the sun go down while you are still angry, and do not give the devil a foothold. Anyone who has been stealing must steal no longer, but must work, doing something useful with their own hands, that they may have something to share with those in need. Do not let any unwholesome talk come out of your mouths, but only what is helpful for building others up according to their needs, that it may benefit those who listen. And do not grieve the Holy Spirit of God, with whom you were sealed for the day of redemption. Get rid of all bitterness, rage and anger, brawling and slander, along with every form of malice" Ephesians 4:26–31.

This is so hard! But it doesn't mean I won't let those words soak into my soul and say, "Lord I receive that over my life with my kids."

"Is there an area of your life where you feel your patience run out fast and become angry?" Take some time to take authority over that. Write and confess your anger then ask God for forgiveness and to show you a way to move past that. Search the word patience in the Bible and commit that to this anger you are feeling.

Self-doubt

I am constantly second guessing myself, even when deep down I am extremely confident in my abilities. I know what I am good at, but I easily cower down to others and hand over credit to other people.

Scripture tells us: "I can do all things though Christ who strengthens me." Philippians 4:13

One of my personal hurdles:

People think I'm weird or that I am socially awkward.

I must force myself to make conversation in groups or crowds. One on one I am fine. Multiple people in a group looking at me, I clam up and say things that I later walk away from going over and over in my head, wondering if I sounded stupid.

"Humble yourselves, therefore, under God's mighty hand, that he may lift you up in due time. Cast all your anxiety on him because he cares for you." 1 Peter 5:6–7

"Am I now trying to win the approval of human beings, or of God? Or am I trying to please people? If I were still trying to please people, I would not be a servant of Christ." Galatians 1:10

What insecurity do face? Take some time to write about that and pray. Give it over to the Lord after you write it out.

_____
_____
_____
_____
_____
_____
_____
_____
_____
_____
_____
_____
_____
_____
_____
_____
_____
_____
_____
_____
_____
_____
_____
_____
_____
_____
_____
_____
_____
_____
_____
_____

Hurdle

Temptation

I enjoy wine and beer. First off let me say, this is not a bad thing. It is not wrong to drink. Nowhere in the Bible does it say, "Do not drink wine or beer." It does, however, say, "Do not get drunk." There are times when I have had one or two and did not want to stop. That's just not healthy. I recognize this and know I need to be careful and not find my identity in it like I used to. I know the devil would like me to indulge whenever I want. I know the lies on this "thing" well. "It's fine, you deserve it," or "You deserve to relax, you work hard."

There are so many verses in the Bible about this, but I'll show you my favorite.

1 Peter 5:8, "Be sober-minded; be watchful. Your adversary the devil prowls around like a roaring lion, seeking someone to devour."

I don't want anything to be more important to me than God, my husband, my kids, or what God might have for me or want me to do. Recognize something that could distance you from the Lord, whatever it might be and choose not to allow that is so important.

"Watch and pray so that you will not fall into temptation. The spirit is willing, but the flesh is weak" (Matt. 26:41).

Through reading this have you thought of another hurdle in your life that you want to hit head on?

Look for words that stand out to you when you write out some hurdles. Then look in the back index of your Bible for those words.

This may bring you to a word search that will help you get through issues in your life. For me, when I was letting go of my past I needed to cut soul ties I had from previous relationships in college. So I looked up *every verse* in the Bible that talked about the soul and found immense healing through that word search.

Hurdle: _____
_____

Bible verse: _____
_____

Hurdle: _____
_____

Bible verse: _____
_____

Now I would like to talk about waiting on God and patience.

Who likes to wait? No one. We get what we want when we want, or at least in two days with a Prime membership.

There have been so many instances in my life when I had to wait. I hated it. I got mad at God in one time of waiting and really questioned Him. That is because I was holding all the control. I was praying so hard, boarder line demanding, that God would change my circumstances. This was hard, to say the least. However, it made me grow! If you handed a child what they asked for instantly every time, would they appreciate that gift? Would they grow? No.

Choosing to wait is really choosing to believe Jesus has a better way than your proposed plan. Do not give up on your desires. Do not choose a different quick path and convince yourself it's the right one because you just cannot wait any longer.

There was a season in my life when I was praying desperately not to be at a job that I had a difficult time going to every day. It took six years until that change finally happened. I kept applying for other jobs and getting no for an answer. However, now I see that had to happen to lead me to the best that God had for me. In those moments, I was so discouraged, angry and sad. But after that season was over, the "why" was revealed. I say this to encourage you to wait so that you can grow in Him and see all He has for you. It may be ten years or one month…only God knows the timings of things.

Before I met my husband, I was painfully single. That deep-down ache and longing feeling was my every day. Finally, I said to the Lord, "God if it's just you and me in this life, I'm okay with it. It's not what I want, I want to have a companion, but I trust you and I will be okay with it, if it is your plan for me to be alone." A few months later, I met my husband. I truly believe that because I released control fully and honestly to the Lord, that fulfilment came.

If you are in this season of waiting, I encourage you to stay strong. Don't go negative with your words as that can speak life or death over a situation. Do not give up, give in or settle. Go for your goals, stay driven, but still wait on God's timing. If you get a lot of no's when you were certain it was the time for a yes, trust Him and praise Him even when you are sad.

Proverbs 18:21 says, "Death and life are in the power of the tongue; and those to whom it is dear will have its fruit for their food."

Honestly, I'm in a new season of waiting right now. My husband is pursuing his passion in life as a career, but it's not a career yet. I believe in him and his talents, and I know it is his calling; so we pursue, and we wait. In the past, this would have been very difficult for me. However, I truly trust God and know that I need to follow Him and rest in that. There is no time table.

"Consider it pure joy, my brothers and sisters, whenever you face trials of many kinds, because you know that the testing of your faith produces perseverance. Let perseverance finish its work so that you may be mature and complete, not lacking anything. If any of you lacks wisdom, you should ask God, who gives generously to all without finding fault, and it will be given to you. But when you ask, you must believe and not doubt, because the one who doubts is like a wave of the sea, blown and tossed by the wind. That person should not expect to receive anything from the Lord. Such a person is double-minded and unstable in all they do." *James 1:2–8*

Is there anything you are waiting on or have had to wait on in the past? Write it below and trust God has the answer in His timing for you.

Okay, ladies, let's talk about RESPONSIBILITY.

"In the same way, older women are to be reverent in behavior, not slanderers, not slaves to excessive drinking. They are to teach what is good, so that they may encourage the young women to love their husbands and to love their children, to be self-controlled, pure, workers at home, kind, and in submission to their husbands, so that God's word will not be slandered". Titus 2: 3-5

We need to take responsibility for our lives. Hustle, hustle go, go, Hustle, hustle go! Did I mention I was a cheerleader? But really let's do this! Clean and declutter your house even if you feel exhausted; rest when you are done. This is a thing for me, so I don't mean to throw it at you. I love a clean home. It makes me feel joyful, rested and peaceful. My husband could take it or leave it, mess does not bother him. But I will literally push myself when I really want to rest, just get it done. Truly, it makes me feel better when I do, so I mention this as encouragement to try it.

I understand there are moments and life circumstances where we need to rest and take care of our health first, and I do not diminish that at all. So if that is the case, then rest first. But get in a general routine of making it a priority to pick up after your home.

I say this because you and your family will feel loved and happy in an orderly place rather than a place of filth and disarray. You need to love yourself enough to take care of yourself and your surroundings. Do not let it go to the wayside because something else was more important. What are some areas in your day to day you'd like to change for the better?

Excuses

We live in a time of making excuses. This is a worldly concept, not a Christlike one. Jesus was an extremely hard worker. We need to follow that example. Try not to get caught up in excuses.

"I'm a hot mess." "I serve at the church and work, so I don't have time for my house." "At least there is food in their mouths." "My kids will remember playing with me, not the mess in here."

Sure, that might be true, but come on, there is time for both! Your kids will respect you and learn a whole lot when they see you clean up and have them help you. Then as a reward, play a game when you are done and/or make cleaning into a dance party! They will be shown task lists through your efforts. It's good for your soul.

I am a full-time working mom that cleans, plays with her kids, cooks' dinner, and co-leads a women's community group/Bible study. It is a part of me, handed down from my dad. He is the guy that is always moving. He was always cleaning, doing yardwork, fixing things and organizing. Really just anything he could find to keep him busy and the house in order. Rarely did I ever see him sit. But when he did finally sit, I remember it was in a clean space. I think seeing this growing up allowed me to have an appreciation for it. I do think it is important to take care of what God has given us.

"Before I formed you in the womb I knew you, and before you were born I consecrated you; I appointed you a prophet to the nations." Then I said, 'Ah, Lord God! Behold, I do not know how to speak, for I am only a youth.' But the Lord said to me, 'Do not say, "I am only a youth"; for to all to whom I send you, you shall go, and whatever I command you, you shall speak. Do not be afraid of them, for I am with you to deliver you, declares the Lord." Jeremiah 1:4–10

Confession—"Lord I need your help in this area of my life. For any excuses I have been making, you see those decisions, and I offer them to you. I want to get stronger and be the woman you designed me."

Division of Women.

"Likewise, teach the older women to be reverent in the way they live, not to be slanderers or addicted to much wine, but to teach what is good. Then they can urge the younger women to love their husbands and children, to be self-controlled and pure, to be busy at home, to be kind, and to be subject to their husbands, so that no one will malign the word of God." Titus 2:3–5

We all find ourselves guilty of thinking, "If we had the money that *they* have and the house that *they* have and the car that *they* have or the marriage that *they* have, then we would be happy." This is a TRAP and not surprisingly it rimes with CRAP. Do not listen to those *lies*; it is straight from the enemy. This one gets a little gumption out of me because I think it is the number one reason for division in the lives of women.

An heiress on earth has no account. We are heiresses of the one and only who has all the accounts. I heard this in a sermon years ago and it has stuck with me ever since.

When you type in heiress in google the "10 richest women in the world" pop up. Being rich is not bad but finding our worth in those riches is bad and will leave you empty. Remember you are an heir of God. The things of this world are not important. The top ten richest people are not important. Your relationship with God is.

Whether you are single, married, kids, no kids, working mom, stay-at-home mom, young or old—we are all equal. Do not let those titles distance you from each other. That is the design of the enemy. Make a choice to be happy for that person, even if you feel pain because you want something they have. Work through it. Be better and trust God for your own life.

We cannot be fake with each other. It is imperative to be vulnerable. Otherwise there will be no growth in our lives. Do not chose who you are real with and who you are not real with. There is a trend in our society to be less and less ourselves and rather to mimic how other (famous) people are. We need to stop this gross cycle and be stronger and be *willing to go to rock bottom to find ourselves.*

Keep it raw because today in our society, "keeping it real" isn't enough. We need to go beyond that. *Go to the raw, painful, depth that so many of us try to keep hidden.*

Once we unearth that depth with friends is when we see church. I found myself at my neighbor's house one weekend. She popped in my mind, so I sent her a text that I would be out and about with my girls on their scooters. She lives down the road and has two girls the same age as mine and told me to come on down! When I got there, I noticed she had a friend over. I immediately apologized and said, "I'm sorry. I didn't realize you had company." She said, "No, girl, this is my best friend. She's been here for a week."

So me being me, I started to try to connect with this friend. I started asking questions; "Where do you live? How do you all know each other. To my surprise she broke down crying and said, "I have nowhere to live and I met her through our husbands. My husband blindsided me this week and asked for a divorce." So now, she said, "I'm left alone and he's breaking up our marriage." She broke down in tears and dropped to the couch with her head in her hands. I asked if I could prayer for her. She said yes. As I sat there crying and praying for her, we had church. That is church. Rallying around your fellow people whether you know them or not does not matter. I felt broken for her and cried with her. The three of us girls sat on the couch and cried and prayed and encouraged each other for hours while our girls played outside.

Take time to journal here about some relationships that need help then lift it up to the Lord in prayer.

Letting Go

I told you about my past. Willing to accept a life that was not mine; I was angry, defeated, and sad. By the grace of God, I found my way back to Him through a very close childhood friend. That was the first step in a long journey. She encouraged me to take a leap of faith and move from Massachusetts to Florida, and it was in Florida that I decided to rededicate my life to the Lord and leave my past emotionally and physically behind. I did just that and chose to pray and ask God for restoration in my life during that year and a half I spent in Florida.

I faced a lot of adversary by people from my high school and college years when I made that decision. Rumors swirled that I had joined a cult! Then when I came home to Massachusetts I faced people telling me that I was basically a hypocrite. It was freaking hard. I was beat down when I was just trying, trying so hard, to make a positive change in my life.

But God continued to put people in my life that would encourage me and mentor me. During this time I met with a woman who lead a Bible study I was attending and she had become a mentor to me. I let her know that I thought my past was not leaving me now that I had moved back to Massachusetts. It was just all flooding back and I didn't think I was strong enough to deal with it. She told me to just take one step at a time. She really broke down the meaning and the truth of the Father, Son, and the Holy Spirit. I was questioning her. "How can there be three?" I said to her. I struggle with believing that. She told me to think about water. Water can be steam, ice, or actual water. It is three things, but they are all the same. Through our conversation it brought me on a beautiful journey with the Lord and truly being able to forgive myself and accepting the Baptism of the Holy Spirit.

Journal something you might be questioning with your faith, then pray and open your Bible.

_____
_____
_____
_____
_____
_____
_____
_____
_____
_____
_____
_____
_____
_____
_____
_____
_____
_____

Now let's dive into taking care of our mind, soul and body. As women, we are masters of criticizing ourselves mentally. This is my number one thing that I need to seek God with, *daily*. We tear ourselves apart in our thought life and as we do that we push God out of the way. Take ownership of that and cast those thoughts down. Speak out loud the truth; *"Lord I know that you have made me in your image, help me to see that every day. I know you love me and love me how I am, help me to be confident in who I am and be unwavering in that."*

Allow the Holy Spirit's authority in your life and recognize you cannot do anything without him when you when you wake up.

Believe God is your healer. Believe God operates through you. You may see a huge bill come in the mail and *think* "there is no way." Change that thought to, "God, I know that you will provide for us. I trust you. Lord, no matter what it might look like, I give you control. I will follow your lead. Please help me in all that I do. Thank you for all you do for me and all you have given to me." It is possible that you may have just made the worst mistake, one you think will wreck your life. So what? *Pray*, ask for forgiveness. Our God is a forgiving God. He's a father to us, and He wants us to come to him in our pain. Kneel to him and confess your sin.

As I conclude this journal, I want to leave you with one last thing. Confidence in God. I struggle with this daily. I mess up every single day. I struggle when I try to find the confidence in myself alone. That's never going to be as good or genuine unless you first find confidence in God. But being reminded that I am loved no matter what and that I need approval from God alone gives me the strength that I need. I know for a fact that I would not be where I am in my life if it weren't for the Lord. Husband, job, house, moving, children, and, honestly, I wouldn't be alive if it weren't for my relationship with the Lord.

We are called to love. It does not matter who we are, what we do, what we *don't* do, we love.

I pray that you love yourself too and go to the Lord for the grace he has for you. Forgive yourself and know that God is bigger than our stupid sins. Each day is a new day, and God's got this and you.

1 Peter 4:8 "Above all, love each other deeply, because love covers over a multitude of sins."

About the Author

A hometown girl from Hudson, Massachusetts, the author Chris Forkuo moved to Thompson's Station, Tennessee, in August 2016, with her husband and two little girls. The country landscapes, beautiful seasons, and people have stolen their hearts. She shares an adventurous spirit and an all-out love for God with her husband. Having a brokenness in her past, Chris came to know who she truly was through Christ. Through that journey, Chris started allowing Christ to lead her steps rather than by herself.

CPSIA information can be obtained
at www.ICGtesting.com
Printed in the USA
LVHW052345100720
660358LV00008B/469

9 781098 004163